MINT

MINT

A BOOK OF RECIPES

HELEN SUDELL

LORENZ BOOKS

This edition published by Lorenz Books
an imprint of Anness Publishing Limited
Blaby Road, Wigston, Leicestershire LE18 4SE
info@anness.com
www.annesspublishing.com
www.lorenzbooks.com

If you like the images in this book and would like to investigate
using them for publishing, promotions or advertising, please visit
our website www.practicalpictures.com for more information

A CIP catalogue record for this book is available from
The British Library

Publisher Joanna Lorenz
Editorial Director Helen Sudell
Designer Nigel Partridge
Illustrations Anna Koska

Photographers: Martin Brigdale, Ian Garlick, Gus Filgate,
William Lingwood, Jon Whitaker, Criag Robertson, Steve Moss,
Nicky Dowey, Polly Wreford
Recipes by: Matthew Drennan, Ghillie Basan, Annette Yates,
Lesley Chamberlain, Sunil Vijayaker, Linda Tubby, Kate Whiteman,
Brian Glover, Judy Bastyra, Jenny White, Alex Barker, Mowie Kay,
Joanna Farrow, Sara Lewis, Tessa Evelegh

COOK'S NOTES

• Bracketed terms are intended for American readers.

• For all recipes, quantities are given in both metric and imperial
measures and, where appropriate, in standard cups and spoons.
Follow one set of measures, but not a mixture, because they are
not interchangeable.

• Standard spoon and cup measures are level. 1 tsp = 5ml,
1 tbsp = 15ml, 1 cup = 250ml/8fl oz.

• Australian standard tablespoons are 20ml. Australian readers
should use 3 tsp in place of 1 tbsp for measuring small quantities.

• American pints are 16fl oz/2 cups. American readers should use
20fl oz/2.5 cups in place of 1 pint when measuring liquids.

• Electric oven temperatures in this book are for conventional
ovens. When using a fan oven, the temperature will probably
need to be reduced by about 10–20°C/20–40°F. Since ovens
vary, you should check with your manufacturer's instruction book
for guidance.

• The nutritional analysis given for each recipe is calculated per
portion (i.e. serving or item), unless otherwise stated. If the recipe
gives a range, such as Serves 4–6, then the nutritional analysis will
be for the smaller portion size, i.e. 6 servings. The analysis does not
include optional ingredients, such as salt added to taste.

• Medium (US large) eggs are used unless otherwise stated.

PUBLISHER'S NOTE

Although the advice and information in this book are believed to
be accurate and true at the time of going to press, neither the
authors nor the publisher can accept any legal responsibility or
liability for any errors or omissions that may have been made nor
for any inaccuracies nor for any loss, harm or injury that comes
about from following instructions or advice in this book.

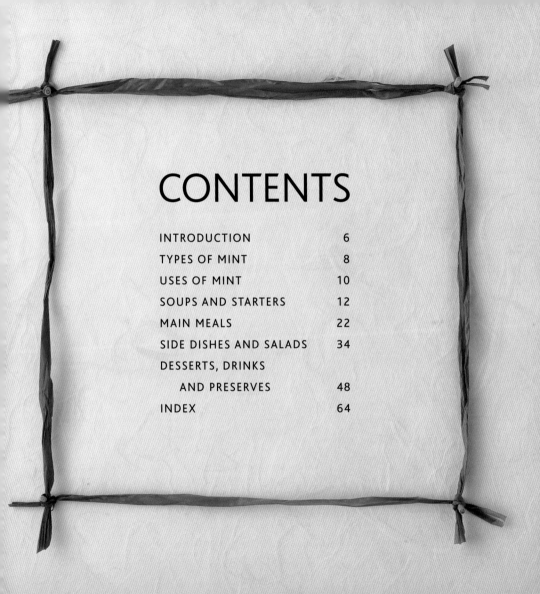

CONTENTS

INTRODUCTION

Mint has been used throughout the world for centuries, not only in cooking but also as a medicine. It was used for many things, ranging from insomnia to poultices for dog bites and bee stings. In the Middle Ages, mint was valued for its refreshing fragrance and used as a strewing herb in churches, banqueting halls and bedrooms, and for scenting baths "as a helpe to comfort and strengthen the nerves and sinewes".

Below: Crush fresh leaves to release their aromatic scent.

A ninth-century monk wrote about the confusing number of mint varieties: "Mints I grow in abundance and in all its varieties. How many there are, I might as well try to count the sparks from Vulcan's furnace beneath Etna." Today, there are about 25 known species.

COOKING WITH MINT

Mint is one of the major aromatics in the cuisines of the Middle East, India and Thailand – just crush a handful of mint and the peppery exotic smell conjures up scenes from an oriental bazaar. The Italians have used mint in their cooking since the days of the Romans, who are thought to have introduced the herb to Britain.

Mint works best with foods that are already inherently sweet. Roast shoulder of lamb with redcurrant jelly and a vinegary mint sauce is a dish made in heaven. Mint goes well with carrots, parsnips, peas and

Above: A sprig of mint adds a colourful, refreshing finish to many fruit desserts.

sweetcorn, and is delicious with fully ripened sliced tomatoes dressed with a drizzle of olive oil and a little black pepper.

It will also happily partner many fruits – mango, spring onion (scallion) and mint is a terrific salsa, or try a fruit salad of Charentais melon, grapes, ginger and mint. Tuck a sprig into a blackberry and apple pie, add it to a quince compote, or even stir it into chocolate mousse to stunning effect.

GROWING AND HARVESTING MINT

Mint always gets out of control if left to its own devices. Even if you hard prune or pull it up, mint always comes back. To prevent rampant root growth, imprison your mint in a large container or earthenware pot embedded in the soil.

When buying mint, choose healthy-looking sprigs with a good fragrance. Avoid wilted specimens with dried ends.

Mint should be harvested just before flowering when the flavour is at its peak. The best

Below: Dry herbs in a cool, airy situation away from sunlight.

time to pick any herb is in the morning after the dew has evaporated but before the sun is too high in the sky.

STORING MINT

Wrap fresh mint in damp kitchen paper and store in a plastic bag in the salad drawer of the refrigerator. Put large bunches in a jug of water and loosely cover with a plastic bag. Keep out of direct sunlight.

Mint is also an easy herb to dry. Tie a handful of mint stalks together with twine and hang upside down until dry. Remove

Above: As mint is fast growing and hard to control, it is best to grow it in containers.

the leaves from the stalk, and store them in an airtight dark glass jar away from direct heat.

If freezing mint, bear in mind that frozen mint is too limp to be used as a garnish but it can be added to soups, sauces and herb butters. Rinse and dry the sprigs and pack them flat in plastic cartons. Snip or grate as required from the frozen clump. Alternatively, chop finely and freeze in ice cube trays.

TYPES OF MINT

Although there are over 25 varieties of mint, the ones listed below are the most commonly available and useful.

SPEARMINT *Mentha spicata*
Also known as garden mint or Moroccan mint, this is the most common variety for cooking. The bright green spear-shaped leaves are deeply veined with toothed edges. They have a strong, clean flavour and are used to season sauces, roast lamb and other meat dishes and vegetables, especially potatoes and peas.

PEPPERMINT *Mentha piperata*
The leaves of the peppermint are a very dark green, and are intensely aromatic. They produce a pungent oil which is used commercially to flavour confectionery, syrups, liqueurs, toothpaste, and medicines. A steam inhalation of the leaves or their oil will alleviate the symptoms of a head cold.

GINGER MINT *Mentha gentilis 'Variegata'*
Ginger mint has smooth variegated leaves splashed with streaks of yellow. The flavour is mysteriously spicy with a hint of ginger, as the name suggests. It is best served as a soothing herbal tea.

BOWLES MINT *Mentha rotundifolia*
A variety of applemint, Bowles mint has apple-scented round, downy leaves with a beautiful flavour. Less assertive than spearmint or peppermint, it is delicious in fruit salads and fruit-based drinks.

CATMINT *Nepeta cataria*
A different genus but from the same family as mint, the plant has coarsely toothed, heart-shaped, grey-green leaves with a pungent scent much loved by cats. The leaves can be rubbed on to meat and young shoots can be used sparingly in salads.

The leaves are rich in vitamin C and an infusion is said to induce sleep.

DRIED MINT
Being pungent and oily, mint dries more successfully and keeps its flavour longer than more delicate herbs. Dried mint can be used in cooking and to make teas. Store it in an airtight dark glass jar away from heat.

MINT JELLY
Traditional mint jelly is good with all kinds of hot or cold meats and poultry, particularly roast lamb.

MINT SAUCE
The acidity of the vinegar in this classic English sauce cuts through the sweetness of lamb.

Dried mint

Mint jelly

Mint sauce

Catmint

Ginger mint

Peppermint

Spearmint

Bowles mint

USES OF MINT

Mint is a natural astringent and fresh or dried mint leaves can be used for a variety of beauty and culinary purposes. If you use fresh leaves, use three times the amount as you would for dried leaves.

BEAUTY
• **Mint and lemon face mask:** Mint leaves can help close up open pores. In a bowl mix one whole egg with 1 tablespoon of

Below: Lemon and mint are often combined in natural skin care treatments, particularly to help treat oily skin.

honey, 1 tablespoon of lemon juice, and 2 tablespoons of chopped fresh mint leaves. Cover your face and neck with the mask and let the mask sit for 15 minutes. Wash off with lukewarm water and pat your face dry with a clean, dry towel.
• **Steam inhalant:** In a bowl steep a large handful of fresh mint leaves in boiling water. Place a towel over your head and breathe in the mint vapours for 10 minutes. Splash your face with cool water to finish.

Above: Mint leaves steeped in boiling water can make a refreshing steam inhalant.

• **Hair rinse:** A mint hair rinse will leave your hair feeling wonderfully smooth and glossy. In a large glass container, mix together equal amounts of chopped mint leaves, water and apple cider vinegar and leave to steep on a sunny windowsill for 3 days. Strain and use immediately by rinsing through newly washed hair.

Above: Mint-flavoured honey is a delicious way to sweeten tea .

Above: Crystallized mint leaves make pretty cake decorations.

MINT SAUCE

The traditional accompaniment to roast lamb, mint sauce is very easy to make at home.

1 Strip a large handful of fresh mint leaves from the stems and chop the leaves very finely.

2 In a pestle and mortar pound the leaves and add 10ml/2 tsp caster (superfine) sugar.

3 Stir in 30ml/2 tbsp boiling water. Add 30ml/2 tbsp cider or white wine vinegar and let it stand for 30 minutes.

CULINARY

• **Mint tea**: Put a large handful of fresh mint leaves in a teapot. Pour over 600 ml/1 pint/2½ cups boiling water, cover and leave for 5 minutes, then strain into cups. Sweeten with honey or sugar if liked.

• **Mint butter**: Cream 115g/4oz/½ cup unsalted butter with 30ml/2 tbsp finely chopped fresh mint, 15ml/1 tbsp lemon juice, and salt and pepper.

• **Mint honey**: Fill a clean glass jar halfway with honey. Add a handful of clean, dry fresh mint leaves, distributing them evenly. Top the rest of the jar up with honey and tighten the lid onto the jar. Allow the mint flavour to steep into the honey and then used as required. Store out of direct sunlight for up to one month.

• **Crystallized mint leaves**: Choose perfect leaves that are completely dry. Lightly whisk egg white until it is just sloppy. With a fine paintbrush, coat the leaves evenly with a thin layer of egg white. Dust lightly with caster (superfine) sugar. Place on a wire rack to dry.

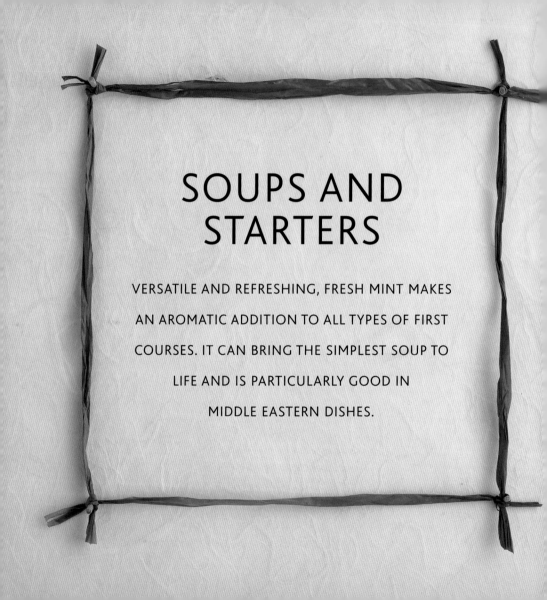

SOUPS AND STARTERS

VERSATILE AND REFRESHING, FRESH MINT MAKES
AN AROMATIC ADDITION TO ALL TYPES OF FIRST
COURSES. IT CAN BRING THE SIMPLEST SOUP TO
LIFE AND IS PARTICULARLY GOOD IN
MIDDLE EASTERN DISHES.

ICED MELON SOUP WITH MELON AND MINT SORBET

Use different melons for the cool soup and ice sorbet to create a subtle contrast in flavour and colour. Try a combination of Charentais and Ogen or Cantaloupe and Galia.

Serves 6–8
2.25kg/5–5¼lb very ripe melon
45ml/3 tbsp orange juice
30ml/2 tbsp lemon juice
mint leaves, to garnish

For the melon and mint sorbet
25g/1oz/2 tbsp sugar
120ml/4fl oz/½ cup water
2.25kg/5–5¼lb very ripe melon
juice of 2 limes
30ml/2 tbsp chopped fresh mint

To make the melon and mint sorbet, put the sugar and water into a saucepan and heat gently until the sugar dissolves. Bring to the boil and simmer for 5 minutes, remove from the heat and leave to cool.

Halve the melon. Scrape out the seeds, and cut the flesh out of the skin. Weigh about 1.5kg/3–3½lb melon. Purée the melon in a blender with the cooled syrup and lime juice.

Stir in the mint and pour the mixture into a suitable container and freeze until icy around the edges. Transfer to a blender and process the mixture until smooth. Repeat the freezing and processing two or three times or until smooth and holding its shape, then freeze until firm.

To make the chilled melon soup, prepare the melon as above and purée it in a blender. Stir in the orange and lemon juice. Place the soup in the refrigerator for 30 minutes. Ladle the soup into bowls and add a large scoop of the sorbet to each. Garnish with mint leaves and serve.

Energy 150kcal/636kJ; Protein 2.9g;
Carbohydrate 35.3g, of which sugars 35.3g;
Fat 0.6g, of which saturates 0g; Cholesterol
0mg; Calcium 75mg; Fibre 2.3g; Sodium
175mg.

MEADOW YOGURT SOUP WITH RICE AND MINT

This is a popular soup all over Turkey. Based on well-flavoured stock and yogurt, it usually contains a little rice and, when flavoured with dried mint, it is called yayla çorbası, *or meadow soup.*

Serves 4

15ml/1 tbsp butter or sunflower oil
1 large onion, finely chopped
scant 15ml/1 tbsp plain (all-purpose) flour
1.2 litres/2 pints/5 cups lamb or chicken stock
75g/3oz/scant ½ cup long grain rice (wild or plain), rinsed
15–30ml/1–2 tbsp dried mint
400ml/14fl oz/1²⁄₃ cups thick and creamy natural (plain) yogurt, strained (see below)
salt and ground black pepper

STRAINING YOGURT

To make strained yogurt, line a sieve (strainer) with a piece of muslin (cheesecloth) and spoon thick and creamy plain yogurt into it. Allow the excess liquid to drip through the muslin, then tip the strained yogurt from the sieve into a bowl.

Melt the butter in a heavy pan, add the onion and cook until soft. Take the pan off the heat and stir in the flour, then pour in the stock, stirring all the time. Return the pan to the heat and bring the stock to the boil, stirring often.

Stir in the rice and most of the mint, reserving a little for the garnish. Lower the heat, cover the pan and simmer for about 20 minutes, until the rice is cooked. Season with salt and pepper.

Beat the yogurt until smooth, then spoon almost all of it into the soup. Keep the heat low and stir vigorously to make sure the yogurt remains smooth and creamy and becomes well blended.

Ladle the soup into bowls, swirl in the remaining yogurt, and garnish with the remaining mint.

Energy 187kcal/781kJ; Protein 7.6g; Carbohydrate 30.3g, of which sugars 11.1g; Fat 4.4g, of which saturates 2.5g; Cholesterol 9mg; Calcium 215mg; Fibre 1g; Sodium 108mg.

PEA AND MINT SOUP

Peas and mint picked fresh from the garden are still true seasonal treats and make a velvety, fresh-tasting soup. Decorate with chive flowers for a special occasion.

Serves 6
25g/1oz/2 tbsp butter
1 medium onion, finely chopped
675g/1½lb shelled fresh peas
1.5ml/¼ tsp sugar
1.2 litres/2 pints/5 cups chicken or vegetable stock
handful of fresh mint leaves
salt and ground black pepper
150ml/¼ pint/⅔ cup double (heavy) cream
snipped fresh chives, to serve

Melt the butter in a large pan and add the onion. Cook over a low heat for about 10 minutes, stirring occasionally, until soft and just brown.

Add the peas, sugar, stock and half the mint. Cover and simmer gently for 10–15 minutes until the peas are tender.

Leave to cool slightly. Add the remaining mint and process or blend until smooth. Return the soup to the pan and season to taste. Stir in the cream and reheat gently without boiling. Serve garnished with snipped chives.

COOK'S TIP
When fresh peas are no longer in season frozen peas may be used instead.

Energy 121kcal/506kJ; Protein 6.1g; Carbohydrate 9.2g, of which sugars 5.2g; Fat 7g, of which saturates 4.2g; Cholesterol 18mg; Calcium 113mg; Fibre 3g; Sodium 123mg.

STUFFED MINTY VINE LEAVES

This vegetarian version of the famous Greek dish uses rice, pine nuts and raisins. The pungency of the mint and parsley add high notes to this comforting dish.

Makes about 40

40 fresh vine leaves
60ml/4 tbsp olive oil
lemon wedges and a crisp salad,
*   to serve*

For the stuffing

30ml/2 tbsp fresh mint leaves
60ml/4 tbsp fresh parsley
150g/5oz/¾ cup long grain
*   rice, rinsed*
2 bunches spring onions
*   (scallions), finely chopped*
40g/1½oz/¼ cup pine nuts
25g/1oz/scant ¼ cup seedless
*   raisins*
3.5ml/¾ tsp freshly ground
*   black pepper*
salt

COOK'S TIP
When fresh vine leaves are unavailable, use 2 packets of vine leaves preserved in brine and rinse then drain well before using.

Using a knife or a pair of scissors, snip out the thick, coarse stems from the vine leaves. Blanch the leaves in a large pan of boiling salted water until they just begin to change colour. Drain and refresh in cold water.

Chop the fresh mint and parsley and mix all the stuffing ingredients together in a bowl.

Open out the vine leaves, ribbed side uppermost. Place a heaped teaspoonful of the stuffing on each.

Fold over the two outer edges to prevent the stuffing from falling out, then roll up the vine leaf from the stem end to form a neat roll.

Arrange the stuffed vine leaves neatly in a steamer and drizzle over the olive oil. Cook over steam for 50–60 minutes, or until the rice is completely cooked. Serve with lemon wedges and a salad, either cold as a meze or hot as a starter to a meal.

Energy 41kcal/169kJ; Protein 1.1g; Carbohydrate 4.7g, of which sugars 1.6g; Fat 2.0g, of which saturates 0.2g; Cholesterol 0mg; Calcium 21mg; Fibre 11.3g; Sodium 3mg

POTATO PAKORAS WITH COCONUT AND MINT SAUCE

These delicious golden bites are sold as street food throughout India. They make a wonderful snack drizzled with the fragrant sauce, or you could sandwich them in a crusty roll for a light lunch.

Makes 25

15ml/1 tbsp sunflower oil
20ml/4 tsp cumin seeds
1 small onion, finely chopped
10ml/2 tsp grated ginger
2 green chillies, chopped
600g/1lb 5oz boiled potatoes
200g/7oz fresh peas
juice of 1 lemon
90ml/6 tbsp chopped fresh
   coriander (cilantro) leaves
115g/4oz/1 cup besan
   (chickpea flour)
65g/2½oz/⅔ cup self-raising
   (self-rising) flour
large pinch of turmeric
350ml/12fl oz/1½ cups water
vegetable oil, for frying
salt and ground black pepper

For the sauce

50g/2oz mint leaves
105ml/7 tbsp coconut cream
200ml/7fl oz/scant 1 cup
   natural (plain) yogurt
5ml/1 tsp golden caster
   (superfine) sugar
juice of 1 lime

Heat a wok over a medium heat and add the sunflower oil. When hot, add the cumin seeds and stir-fry for 1–2 minutes.

Add the onion, ginger and chillies to the wok and cook for 3–4 minutes. Add the cooked potatoes and peas and stir-fry for 3-4 minutes. Season, then stir in the lemon juice and coriander leaves.

Leave the mixture to cool slightly, then divide into 25 portions. Shape each portion into a ball and chill.

To make the batter put the besan and self-raising flour in a bowl. Season and add the turmeric. Gradually whisk in the water to make a smooth, thick batter.

To make the chutney, chop the mint finely and place all the ingredients in a blender and process until smooth. Season, then chill.

To cook the pakoras, fill a wok one-third full of oil and heat to 180°C/350°F. (A cube of bread, dropped into the oil, should brown in 15 seconds.) Working in batches, dip the balls in the batter, then drop into the oil and deep-fry for 1–2 minutes, or until golden. Drain on kitchen paper and serve with the sauce.

Energy 126kcal/525kJ; Protein 4.1g; Carbohydrate 8.3g, of which sugars 2.6g; Fat 8.8g, of which saturates 5.2g; Cholesterol 0mg; Calcium 35mg; Fibre 1.3g; Sodium 16mg.

MAIN MEALS

WITH ITS INTENSE, SWEET AROMA, MINT IS A
DELICIOUS ACCOMPANIMENT TO MANY MAIN
DISHES. IT HAS A SPECIAL AFFINITY WITH LAMB BUT
WORKS EQUALLY WELL WITH CHICKEN, FISH AND
VEGETARIAN DISHES, PARTICULARLY FROM THE
MEDITERRANEAN REGION.

LAMB KEBABS WITH MINT CHUTNEY

These little round lamb kebabs owe their exotic flavour to ras el hanout, a North African spice, which is the best the world can offer. The cooling mint chutney provides the perfect accompaniment.

Serves 4–6

30ml/2 tbsp extra virgin olive oil
1 onion, finely chopped
2 garlic cloves, crushed
35g/1¼oz/5 tbsp pine nuts
500g/1¼lb/2½ cups minced (ground) lamb
10ml/2 tsp ras el hanout spice mix
salt and ground black pepper
18 short wooden or metal skewers

For the fresh mint chutney

40g/1½oz/1½ cups fresh mint leaves
10ml/2 tsp sugar
juice of 2 lemons
2 eating apples, peeled and finely grated

Heat the oil in a frying pan. Add the onion and garlic and fry gently for 5 minutes. Stir in the pine nuts. Fry for about 5 minutes more, or until the mixture is slightly golden, then set aside to cool.

Make the fresh mint chutney. Chop the mint finely, then add the sugar, lemon juice and grated apple. Stir or pulse to mix.

Prepare the barbecue. Place the minced lamb in a large bowl and add the ras el hanout. Tip in the cooled onion mixture and season. Using your hands, mix well, then form into 18 balls and mould them onto skewers. Once the flames have died down, rake a few hot coals to one side. Position a lightly oiled grill rack over the coals to heat.

When the coals have a thick coating of ash, place the kebabs on the grill and cook gently. Serve with the mint chutney and a green salad.

Energy 257kcal/1070kJ; Protein 17.2g;
Carbohydrate 5.1g, of which sugars 4.5g;
Fat 18.8g, of which saturates 6g;
Cholesterol 64mg; Calcium 33mg;
Fibre 0.6g; Sodium 59mg.

ROAST SHOULDER OF LAMB WITH MINT SAUCE

Lamb is a favourite Sunday lunch meal, which is particularly popular at Easter. Mint sauce, with its sweet-sour combination, has been lamb's customary accompaniment since the 17th century.

Serves 6–8

*boned shoulder of lamb,
    weighing 1.5–2kg/3¼–4½lb*
30ml/2 tbsp fresh thyme leaves
30ml/2 tbsp clear honey
*150ml/¼ pint/⅔ cup dry (hard)
    cider or white wine*
*30–45ml/2–3 tbsp double
    (heavy) cream (optional)*
salt and ground black pepper

For the mint sauce

*large handful of fresh mint
    leaves*
*15ml/1 tbsp caster (superfine)
    sugar*
*45–60ml/3–4 tbsp cider vinegar
    or wine vinegar*

Preheat the oven to 220°C/425°F/Gas 7. To make the mint sauce, finely chop the mint leaves with the sugar (the sugar draws the juices from the mint) and put the mixture into a bowl.

Add 30ml/2 tbsp boiling water to the mint and sugar, and stir well until the sugar has dissolved. Add the vinegar to taste and leave the sauce to stand for at least 1 hour for the flavours to blend.

Open out the lamb with skin side down. Season with salt and pepper, sprinkle with the thyme leaves and drizzle the honey over the top. Roll up and tie securely with string in several places. Place the meat in a roasting pan and put into the hot oven. Cook for 30 minutes until browned all over.

Pour the cider and 150ml/¼ pint/⅔ cup water into the tin. Lower the oven to 160°C/325°F/Gas 3 and cook for about 45 minutes for medium (pink) or about 1 hour for well-done meat.

Remove the lamb from the oven, cover loosely with a sheet of foil and leave to stand for 20–30 minutes.

Lift the lamb on to a warmed serving plate. Skim any excess fat from the surface of the pan juices before reheating and seasoning to taste. Stir in the cream, if using, bring to the boil and remove from the heat. Carve the lamb and serve it with the pan juices spooned over, and the mint sauce.

Energy 351kcal/1468kJ; Protein 36.9g;
Carbohydrate 2.5g, of which sugars 2.5g;
Fat 21g, of which saturates 9.8g;
Cholesterol 143mg; Calcium 23mg;
Fibre 0g; Sodium 202mg

BULGUR AND SPICY LAMB WITH MINT

This dish is originally from Turkey where it is served with plain yogurt and lemon slices, or cacik, a refreshing cucumber, mint and yogurt salad (see page 41).

Serves 4

30ml/2 tbsp ghee, or butter
2 onions, chopped
10ml/2 tsp sugar
350g/12oz bulgur wheat, rinsed
     and drained
10ml/2 tsp tomato purée
     (paste)
600ml/1 pint/2½ cups lamb or
     chicken stock, or water
10ml/2 tsp paprika
5–10ml/1–2 tsp ground cumin
5ml/1 tsp ground coriander
250g/9oz shoulder of lamb, cut
     into bitesize pieces
salt and ground black pepper
fresh mint sprigs, chopped, to
     garnish
natural (plain) yogurt and
     lemon slices, to serve

Energy 541kcal/2259kJ; Protein 21.1g;
Carbohydrate 86.1g, of which sugars 9g;
Fat 15g, of which saturates 7.2g;
Cholesterol 64mg; Calcium 49mg;
Fibre 3.3g; Sodium 110mg.

Melt the ghee or butter in a heavy pan. Stir in the onion with the sugar and fry gently for 3–4 minutes, or until golden brown.

Toss in the bulgur wheat, coating it in the onion and ghee, and stir in the tomato purée.

Pour in the stock or water, season, and bring it to the boil. Reduce the heat and simmer until all the water has been absorbed. Turn the heat off, cover the pan with a clean dish towel, place the lid on firmly, and leave to steam for 10–15 minutes.

Put the spices and lamb pieces in a plastic bag and shake to coat. Heat a wide, heavy, non-stick frying pan. Toss the meat quickly on its own in the pan, frying it in its own juices, until it is lightly browned.

Add the bulgur wheat to the pan with the meat, and toss both around the pan for 2–3 minutes, or until the flavours are thoroughly mixed.

Transfer the bulgur wheat and lamb to a serving dish, garnish with the chopped mint and serve hot with lemon slices or yogurt.

FRAGRANT RICE WITH CHICKEN AND MINT

From the north of Vietnam, where fresh herbs play an important role in the cuisine, this refreshing rice dish can be served very simply, or as part of a larger meal with fish or chicken.

Serves 4

350g/12oz/1¾ cups long grain rice, rinsed and drained
2–3 shallots, halved and finely sliced
1 bunch of fresh mint, stalks removed, leaves finely shredded
2 spring onions (scallions), finely sliced, to garnish

For the stock

2 meaty chicken legs
1 onion, peeled and quartered
4cm/1½in fresh root ginger, peeled and coarsely chopped
15ml/1 tbsp nuoc mam
3 black peppercorns
1 bunch of fresh mint
sea salt

To make the stock, put the chicken legs into a deep pan. Add all the other ingredients, except the salt, and pour in 1 litre/1¾ pints/4 cups water. Bring the water to the boil, skim off any foam, then reduce the heat and simmer gently with the lid on for 1 hour. Remove the lid, increase the heat and simmer for a further 30 minutes to reduce the stock. Skim off any fat, strain the stock and season with salt. Measure 750ml/1¼ pints/3 cups stock. Remove the chicken meat from the bone and shred.

Put the rice in a heavy pan and stir in the stock. When the rice settles, check that the stock sits roughly 2.5cm/1in above the rice; if not, top it up. Bring the liquid to the boil, cover the pan and cook for about 25 minutes, or until all the water has been absorbed.

Remove the pan from the heat and, using a fork, add the shredded chicken, shallots and most of the mint. Cover the pan again and leave the flavours to mingle for 10 minutes. Tip the rice into bowls, or on to a serving dish, and garnish with the remaining mint and the spring onions.

Energy 370kcal/1569kJ; Protein 12g; Carbohydrate 79g, of which sugars 1g; Fat 3g, of which saturates 0g; Cholesterol 26mg; Calcium 41mg; Fibre 0.8g; Sodium 200mg.

HOKI FISH CURRY WITH HERBS

Hoki is an ideal firm-fleshed fish to use for this delicious curry, which gains its rich colour from a mixture of fresh herbs. Serve it with basmati or Thai fragrant rice and lime wedges.

Serves 4

2 red onions, finely chopped
900g/2lb hoki fillets, skinned
400ml/14fl oz/1²/₃ cups
coconut milk
45ml/3 tbsp Thai fish sauce
50g/2oz/1 cup fresh coriander
(cilantro) leaves
50g/2oz/1 cup fresh mint leaves
50g/2oz/1 cup fresh basil leaves
6 spring onions (scallions),
chopped
150ml/¼ pint/²/₃ cup sunflower
or groundnut (peanut) oil
sliced fresh green chilli and
chopped coriander, to garnish
cooked basmati or Thai fragrant
rice and lime wedges, to serve

For the curry paste

4 garlic cloves, chopped
5cm/2in piece fresh root ginger,
2 fresh green chillies, chopped
grated rind and juice of 1 lime
5ml/1 tsp coriander seeds
5ml/1 tsp Chinese five-spice
powder
75ml/5 tbsp sesame oil

First make the curry paste. Peel and coarsely chop the ginger. Combine the garlic, fresh root ginger, green chillies, and the lime juice in a food processor. Add the coriander seeds and five-spice powder, with half the sesame oil. Process to a fine paste, then set aside until required.

Heat a wok or large shallow pan and pour in the remaining sesame oil. When it is hot, stir-fry the red onions over a high heat for 2 minutes. Add the fish and stir-fry for 1–2 minutes to seal the fillets on all sides.

Lift out the red onions and fish and put them on a plate. Add the curry paste to the wok or pan and fry for 1 minute, stirring. Return the hoki fillets and red onions to the wok or pan, pour in the coconut milk and bring to the boil. Lower the heat, add the fish sauce and simmer for 5–7 minutes, until the fish is cooked through.

Meanwhile, process the herbs, spring onions, lime rind and oil in a food processor to a coarse paste. Stir into the fish curry. Garnish with chilli and coriander and serve with rice and lime wedges.

Energy 575kcal/2390kJ; Protein 40g; Carbohydrate 6.2g, of which sugars 4.9g; Fat 43.5g, of which saturates 5.9g; Cholesterol 6mg; Calcium 132mg; Fibre 0g; Sodium 362mg.

AUBERGINE PILAFF WITH CINNAMON AND MINT

This wonderful Turkish rice dish is full of flavour. Eat it on its own accompanied by a green salad, or serve it with grilled, broiled or barbecued meat.

Serves 4–6

2 large aubergines (eggplants)
30–45ml/2–3 tbsp olive oil
30–45ml/2–3 tbsp pine nuts
1 large onion, finely chopped
5ml/1 tsp coriander seeds
30ml/2 tbsp currants, soaked in
   warm water for 5–10 minutes
   and drained
10–15ml/2–3 tsp sugar
15–30ml/1–2 tbsp ground
   cinnamon
15–30ml/1–2 tbsp dried mint
1 small bunch of fresh dill, finely
   chopped
3 tomatoes, skinned, seeded
   and finely chopped
350g/12oz/generous 1¾ cups
   long or short grain rice, well
   rinsed and drained
sunflower oil, for deep-frying
juice of ½ lemon
salt and ground black pepper
fresh mint sprigs and lemon
   wedges, to serve

Using a vegetable peeler or a small, sharp knife, peel the aubergines lengthways in stripes like a zebra. Quarter them lengthways, then slice each quarter into bitesize chunks and place in a bowl of salted water. Cover with a plate to keep them submerged, and leave to soak for at least 30 minutes.

Meanwhile, heat the olive oil in a heavy pan, stir in the pine nuts and cook until they turn golden. Add the onion and soften it, then stir in the coriander seeds and currants. Add the sugar, cinnamon, mint and dill and stir in the tomatoes.

Toss in the rice, coating it well in the tomato and spices, then pour in 900ml/1½ pints/3¾ cups water, season with salt and pepper and bring to the boil. Lower the heat and partially cover the pan, then simmer for 10–12 minutes, until almost all of the water has been absorbed. Turn off the heat, cover the pan with a dish towel and press the lid tightly on top. Leave the rice to steam for about 15 minutes.

Heat enough sunflower oil for deep-frying in a wok or other deep-sided pan. Drain the aubergines and squeeze them dry, then toss them in batches in the oil, for a few minutes at a time. When they are golden brown, lift them out with a slotted spoon and drain on kitchen paper.

Tip the rice into a serving bowl and toss the aubergine chunks through it with the lemon juice. Garnish with fresh mint sprigs and serve warm or cold, with lemon wedges for squeezing.

Energy 369kcal/1539kJ; Protein 6.1g; Carbohydrate 52.2g, of which sugars 11g; Fat 15.2g, of which saturates 1.8g; Cholesterol 0mg; Calcium 38mg; Fibre 2.7g; Sodium 8mg.

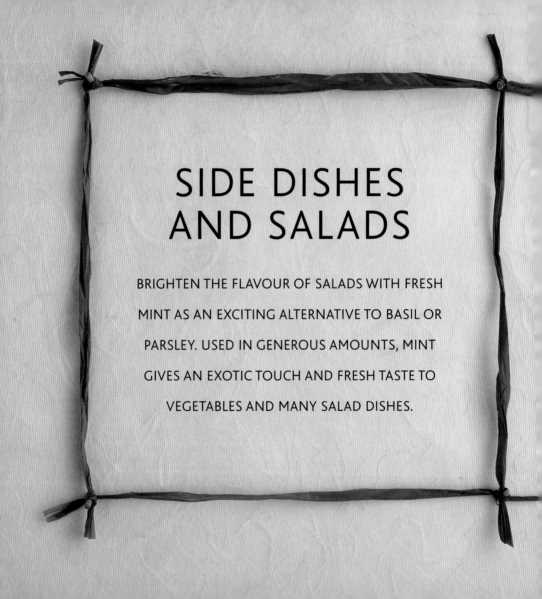

SIDE DISHES
AND SALADS

BRIGHTEN THE FLAVOUR OF SALADS WITH FRESH
MINT AS AN EXCITING ALTERNATIVE TO BASIL OR
PARSLEY. USED IN GENEROUS AMOUNTS, MINT
GIVES AN EXOTIC TOUCH AND FRESH TASTE TO
VEGETABLES AND MANY SALAD DISHES.

BRAISED LETTUCE AND PEAS WITH MINT

This is based on the traditional French way of braising peas with lettuce, mint and spring onions (scallions) in butter. It is delicious with simply cooked fish or roast or grilled duck.

Serves 4

50g/2oz/¼ cup butter
4 Little Gem (Bibb) lettuces, halved lengthways
2 bunches spring onions, (scallions), trimmed
5ml/1 tsp caster (superfine) sugar
400g/14oz shelled peas (about 1kg/2¼lb in pods)
4 fresh mint sprigs
120ml/4fl oz/½ cup chicken or vegetable stock or water
15ml/1 tbsp chopped fresh mint, to serve
salt and ground black pepper

Melt half the butter in a wide, heavy-based saucepan over a low heat. Add the lettuce and spring onions.

Turn the vegetables in the butter, then sprinkle in the sugar, 2.5ml/½ tsp salt and plenty of black pepper. Cover, and cook very gently for 5 minutes, stirring once.

Add the peas and mint sprigs. Turn the peas in the buttery juices and pour in the stock or water, then cover and cook over a gentle heat for a further 5 minutes. Uncover and increase the heat to reduce the liquid to a few tablespoons.

Stir in the remaining butter and adjust the seasoning. Transfer to a warmed serving dish, sprinkle with the chopped mint and serve.

Energy 161kcal/670kJ; Protein 9.1g;
Carbohydrate 15.9g, of which sugars 6.8g;
Fat 7.4g, of which saturates 3.7g;
Cholesterol 13mg; Calcium 73mg;
Fibre 6.5g; Sodium 47mg.

ROASTED COURGETTES WITH VINEGAR AND MINT

The courgette (zucchini) is a very popular vegetable in the eastern Mediterranean region. This recipe makes a lovely side dish for grilled or roasted meats and fish.

Serves 4–6

4–6 courgettes (zucchini), trimmed and sliced lengthways
4 cloves garlic, halved and lightly crushed
45–60ml/3–4 tbsp olive oil
30ml/2 tbsp cider or white wine vinegar
10ml/2 tsp dried mint
sea salt

Preheat the oven to 180°C/350°F/Gas 4. Place the courgette slices in an ovenproof dish with the garlic cloves.

Pour the olive oil over the courgettes, and roast in the oven for 25–30 minutes, until softened and lightly browned.

Lift the courgette slices and some of the garlic out of the dish and arrange on a warmed serving plate. Mix 30–45ml/2–3 tbsp of the cooking oil with the vinegar and dried mint and drizzle it over the courgettes. Sprinkle with salt and serve warm or at room temperature.

Energy 78kcal/322kJ; Protein 2.7g;
Carbohydrate 3.3g, of which sugars 2.1g;
Fat 6g, of which saturates 0.9g;
Cholesterol 0mg; Calcium 36mg;
Fibre 1.3g; Sodium 2mg

BROAD BEANS WITH BACON AND MINT

In early summer, tender young broad (fava) beans are a treat, and fresh mint and a smattering of crisply cooked bacon are their perfect partners. Frozen broad beans can also work equally well.

Serves 4–6

30ml/2 tbsp olive oil
175g/6oz streaky (fatty) bacon,
    cut into narrow strips
1 medium onion, thinly sliced
2.5ml/½ tsp sugar
450g/1lb shelled broad (fava)
    beans
15ml/1 tbsp cider vinegar
small handful of fresh mint,
    finely chopped
salt and ground black pepper

COOK'S TIP
Serve warm or at room temperature as a salad with crusty bread, or hot as an accompaniment to roast duck or chicken.

Energy 162kcal/674kJ; Protein 7.9g;
Carbohydrate 9.6g, of which sugars 1.8g;
Fat 10.5g, of which saturates 2.2g;
Cholesterol 9mg; Calcium 45mg;
Fibre 4.5g; Sodium 190mg

Heat half the oil in a large pan and cook the bacon until crisp. Lift out with a slotted spoon and set aside.

Add the onion to the hot pan with the sugar and cook over a medium heat until soft and golden brown.

Meanwhile, bring a pan of water to the boil and add the beans. Cook for 5–8 minutes until tender. Drain well.

Add the cooked beans and bacon to the onions. Stir in the remaining oil, vinegar, mint and seasonings and serve.

SWEET-AND-SOUR CUCUMBER WITH CHILLIES AND HERBS

This classic Vietnamese salad features cucumbers dressed with lime and herbs to make a delightful accompaniment to meat, poultry and seafood dishes.

Serves 4–6

2 cucumbers

30ml/2 tbsp caster (superfine) sugar

100ml/3½fl oz/scant ½ cup rice vinegar

juice of half a lime

1–2 green Thai chillies, seeded and finely sliced

2 shallots, halved and finely sliced

1 small bunch each of fresh coriander (cilantro) and mint, stalks removed, leaves finely chopped

salt

Use a vegetable peeler to remove strips of the cucumber peel. Halve the cucumber lengthways and cut into slices. Place the slices on a plate and sprinkle with a little salt. Leave to stand for 15 minutes, then rinse and drain.

In a bowl, mix the sugar with the vinegar until it has dissolved, then stir in the lime juice and a little salt to taste.

Add the chillies, shallots, herbs and cucumber to the dressing, mix well and leave to stand for 15–20 minutes to allow the flavours to mingle before serving.

Energy 59Kcal/248kJ; Protein 2g; Carbohydrate 12g, of which sugars 11g Fat 0g, of which saturates 0g; Cholesterol 0mg; Cacium 63mg; Fibre 0.8g; Sodium 0.2g

RICE WITH GREEN PEAS, MINT AND DILL

This plain buttery pilaff is delicious when served with fried or grilled chicken and fish dishes. It also makes an attractive addition to a buffet spread or barbecue.

Serves 4

15ml/1 tbsp olive oil
25g/1oz/2 tbsp butter
1 onion, finely chopped
350g/12oz/1¾ cups long grain rice, thoroughly rinsed and drained
750ml/1¼ pints/3 cups chicken stock or water
200g/7oz/1¾ cups fresh or frozen peas
1 small bunch dill, finely chopped
1 small bunch mint, leaves finely chopped
salt and ground black pepper

Energy 437kcal/1819kJ; Protein 10.5g;
Carbohydrate 77g, of which sugars 2.3g;
Fat 9.3g, of which saturates 3.8g;
Cholesterol 13mg; Calcium 57mg;
Fibre 3.2g; Sodium 43mg.

Heat the oil and butter in a heavy pan and stir in the onion. Cook until softened. Add the rice, coating it in the butter and onion, and pour in the stock or water.

Season and bring the stock to the boil. Reduce the heat and simmer for 10 minutes, or until almost all the liquid has been absorbed.

Toss the peas into the rice with half the fresh herbs. Cover the pan with a clean dish towel and a lid and leave the rice to steam with the peas for a further 10 minutes.

Transfer the cooked rice mixture to a serving dish, garnish with the remaining fresh herbs, and serve the pilaff hot or at room temperature.

CUCUMBER AND MINT SALAD

Refreshing and versatile, this dish can be served as a salad or as an accompaniment. In Turkey, this salad is called cacik *and is often served as a cooling accompaniment to spicy kebabs.*

Serves 4

1 large cucumber or 2 small ones
500g/1¼lb thick and creamy natural (plain) yogurt
2 garlic cloves, crushed
1 bunch fresh mint, leaves chopped
olive oil, for drizzling
salt and ground black pepper

Using a vegetable peeler, partially peel the cucumber skin in stripes. Cut the cucumber in half lengthways and slice it finely.

Place the slices in a colander and sprinkle with salt. Leave to weep for 5–10 minutes. Rinse the sliced cucumber and drain well.

In a wide bowl, beat the yogurt with the garlic and most of the mint. Add the sliced cucumber and season to taste.

Transfer to a serving bowl, drizzle a little olive oil over the top and garnish with the remaining chopped mint.

Serve with chunks of fresh bread and other meze dishes.

COOK'S TIPS
• As a meze dish, you can slice, dice or grate the cucumber, depending on your own personal preference.
• It can be flavoured with fresh or dried mint or with fresh dill.

Energy 83kcal/348kJ; Protein 7.4g;
Carbohydrate 11.2g, of which sugars 10.1g;
Fat 1.4g, of which saturates 0.6g;
Cholesterol 2mg; Calcium 273mg;
Fibre 0.4g; Sodium 107mg.

MEDITERRANEAN SALAD WITH HERBS

Each region of the eastern Mediterranean has its own version of this classic salad. This is a typical, everyday, country salad that originates from the Lebanon.

Serves 4–6

1 cos or romaine lettuce
1 cucumber
2 tomatoes
2–3 spring onions (scallions)
bunch of fresh mint leaves
bunch of flat leaf parsley
30ml/2 tbsp olive oil
juice of ½ lemon
sea salt

Cut the lettuce leaves into bitesize chunks and place in a bowl. Partially peel the cucumber and cut into small chunks, skin the tomatoes and dice the flesh. Trim and slice the spring onions and add all the vegetables to the bowl.

Wash and finely chop the mint and parsley, discarding the stalks, and add to the vegetables. Toss all the ingredients together in the olive oil and lemon juice. Sprinkle with salt and serve.

COOK'S TIP
This salad can be served as an accompaniment to many Lebanese dishes, as well as part of a larger meze spread.

Energy 51kcal/210kJ; Protein 1.1g;
Carbohydrate 2.5g, of which sugars 2.4g;
Fat 4.1g, of which saturates 0.6g;
Cholesterol 0mg; Calcium 36mg;
Fibre 1.3g; Sodium 8mg

CHICKPEA AND BULGUR SALAD WITH MINT

This fragrant vegetarian salad uses simple ingredients bound with olive oil and lemon juice and tossed with lots of freshly chopped mint and parsley.

Serves 4–6

150g/5oz/scant 1 cup fine bulgur wheat, rinsed
15–30ml/1–2 tbsp sesame seeds
400g/14oz canned chickpeas, drained and rinsed
1 red onion, finely chopped
2–3 cloves garlic, crushed
60–75ml/4–5 tbsp olive oil
juice of 1–2 lemons
bunch of flatleaf parsley, finely chopped
large bunch of mint, coarsely chopped
sea salt and ground black pepper
5ml/1 tsp paprika, to garnish

Place the bulgur in a bowl and pour over boiling water to cover. Leave to soak for 10–15 minutes, until it has doubled in volume.

Meanwhile, toast the sesame seeds. Heat a frying pan and pour in enough seeds to just cover the bottom of the pan. Dry-fry the seeds over a low heat, stirring constantly, until they turn golden brown. Then place the chickpeas in a bowl with the onion, toasted sesame seeds and garlic and bind with the olive oil and lemon juice.

Squeeze the bulgur to remove any excess water and add it to the chickpeas with the parsley and mint. Toss well, season with salt and pepper to taste, and sprinkle the paprika over the top.

Energy 267kcal/1116kJ; Protein 8.6g; Carbohydrate 34.1g, of which sugars 3.3g; Fat 11.4g, of which saturates 1.4g; Cholesterol 0mg; Calcium 89mg; Fibre 4.1g; Sodium 153mg

GRILLED AUBERGINE, MINT AND COUSCOUS SALAD

The beauty of this simple salad is that it looks and tastes so good and yet has few ingredients and takes minutes to make. It is best served with a crisp green salad.

Serves 2
1 large aubergine (eggplant)
45ml/3 tbsp olive oil
salt and ground black pepper
3 garlic cloves
30ml/2 tbsp chopped fresh
* coriander (cilantro)*
115g/4oz packet couscous
30ml/2 tbsp chopped fresh mint

COOK'S TIP
If you prefer, you can buy ready-flavoured couscous from most supermarkets. There are different flavours available, but garlic and coriander is particularly good for this recipe.

Energy 251kcal/1044kJ; Protein 4.8g;
Carbohydrate 32.5g, of which sugars 2g;
Fat 12.1g, of which saturates 1.7g;
Cholesterol 0mg; Calcium 53mg;
Fibre 2g; Sodium 5mg

Preheat the grill (broiler) to high. Cut the aubergine into large chunky pieces and toss them with 30ml/2 tbsp of the olive oil. Season with salt and pepper to taste and spread the aubergine pieces on a non-stick baking sheet. Grill for 5–6 minutes, turning occasionally, until golden brown.

Meanwhile, prepare the couscous. Finely chop the garlic and fry gently in 15ml/1 tbsp olive oil until golden. Cook the couscous according to the instructions on the packet and add the garlic and chopped coriander to flavour the couscous. Stir the grilled aubergine and chopped mint into the couscous, toss thoroughly and serve immediately.

DESSERTS, DRINKS AND PRESERVES

THE DIGESTIVE PROPERTIES OF MINT MAKE IT IDEAL

TO ROUND OFF A MEAL. USED SPARINGLY, IT CAN

ADD AN UNEXPECTED BURST OF FLAVOUR TO FRUIT

DESSERTS AND IS EXCELLENT WHEN COMBINED

WITH CHOCOLATE AND CREAM.

MINTED POMEGRANATE YOGURT AND GRAPEFRUIT SALAD

In this Moroccan dessert rich ruby pomegranate seeds add texture, flavour and colour to a
deceptively simple dish. It is fabulous served with a delicately scented citrus fruit salad.

Serves 3–4

300ml/½ pint/1¼ cups Greek
(US strained plain) yogurt
2–3 ripe pomegranates
small bunch of mint, finely
chopped
honey or sugar, to taste
(optional)

For the grapefruit salad

2 red grapefruits
2 pink grapefruits
1 white grapefruit
15–30ml/1–2 tbsp orange
flower water
handful of pomegranate seeds
and mint leaves, to decorate

Put the yogurt in a bowl and beat well. Cut open the pomegranates and scoop out the seeds, removing all the bitter pith. Fold most of the pomegranate seeds and chopped mint into the yogurt. Sweeten with a little honey or sugar, if using, then chill until ready to serve.

Peel the red, pink and white grapefruits, cutting off all the pith. Cut between the membranes to remove the segments, holding the fruit over a bowl to catch the juices.

Discard the membranes and mix the fruit segments with the reserved juices. Sprinkle with the orange flower water and add a little honey or sugar, if using.

Decorate the chilled yogurt with a scattering of pomegranate seeds and mint leaves, and serve with the grapefruit salad.

Energy 188kcal/784kJ; Protein 8.8g;
Carbohydrate 18g, of which sugars 18g;
Fat 10.5g, of which saturates 5.2g;
Cholesterol 0mg; Calcium 202mg;
Fibre 3.6g; Sodium 82mg.

MINT CHOC BROWNIES

Chocolate and mint make a marvellous combination, but it's unusual to find them in a cake. Here brownies contain crisp pieces of peppermint and are covered with a minty buttercream topping.

Makes 25

75g/3oz/¾ cup unsweetened
    cocoa powder
75g/3oz clear peppermint
    boiled sweets (hard candies)
275g/10oz/2½ cups plain
    (all-purpose) flour
7.5ml/1½ tsp bicarbonate of
    soda (baking soda)
2.5ml/½ tsp baking powder
175g/6oz/¾ cup soft tub
    margarine, plus extra for
    greasing
275g/10oz/scant 1½ cups soft
    dark brown sugar
3 eggs, beaten

For the topping

115g/4oz/½ cup unsalted
    (sweet) butter, softened
225g/8oz/2 cups icing
    (confectioners') sugar
30ml/2 tbsp milk
2.5ml/½ tsp peppermint extract
a few drops of green food
    colouring
thin chocolate mint sticks

Dissolve the cocoa powder in 350ml/12fl oz/1½ cups boiling water, stir, then leave for 30 minutes.

Preheat the oven to 180°C/350°F/Gas 4. Grease and line a 23cm/9in square deep cake tin (pan) with baking parchment.

Put the boiled mints into a strong plastic bag and tap with a rolling pin until they break into small pieces.

Sift the flour, bicarbonate of soda and baking powder into the cocoa.

Add the margarine, sugar and eggs and beat for 2 minutes. Fold in the crushed mints and spoon into the tin. Smooth the top level.

Bake for 1 hour 10 minutes, or until baked through. Allow to cool in the tin.

To make the topping, beat the butter with the icing sugar, milk, peppermint extract and a few drops of green food colouring. Spread over the cooled cake.

Cut into squares and decorate each with two chocolate mint sticks.

Energy 331kcal/1379kJ; Protein 3.8g; Carbohydrate 30.2g, of which sugars 21.4g; Fat 22.5g, of which saturates 6.7g; Cholesterol 49mg; Calcium 37mg; Fibre 1.1g; Sodium 50mg.

MINT CHOCOLATE MERINGUES

These mini meringues are perfect for a child's birthday party and could be tinted pink or green. Any spares are delicious crunched into your next batch of vanilla ice cream.

Makes about 50
2 egg whites
115g/4oz/generous ½ cup caster (superfine) sugar
50g/2oz chocolate mint sticks, chopped
cocoa powder, sifted (optional)

For the filling
150ml/¼ pint/⅔ cup double (heavy) or whipping cream
5–10ml/1–2 tsp crème de menthe, or mint extract

Preheat the oven to 110°C/225°F/Gas ¼. Whisk the egg whites until stiff, then gradually whisk in the sugar until thick and glossy. Fold in the chopped mint sticks and then place teaspoons of the mixture on baking sheets covered with non-stick baking paper.

Bake for 1 hour or until crisp. Remove from the oven and allow to cool, then dust with cocoa, if using.

Lightly whip the cream, stir in the crème de menthe, and sandwich the meringues together just before serving.

Energy 30kcal/123kJ; Protein 0.2g; Carbohydrate 3.1g, of which sugars 3.1g; Fat 1.9g, of which saturates 1.2g; Cholesterol 4mg; Calcium 3mg; Fibre 0g; Sodium 3mg.

COOK'S TIP
You can store these meringues in airtight tins or jars; they will keep for several days.

MINT AND CHOCOLATE MINI WHOOPIE PIES

The classic combination of mint and chocolate works beautifully in these decadent whoopie pies.
For a stronger minty flavour, chop some dark mint chocolates and add to the buttercream filling.

Makes 24

For the cakes
125g/4¼oz/8½ tbsp unsalted (sweet) butter, softened
175g/6oz/¾ cup soft light brown sugar
seeds of 1 vanilla pod (bean)
1 egg
300g/11oz/2¾ cups plain (all-purpose) flour
40g/1½oz cocoa powder
7.5ml/1½ tsp bicarbonate of soda (baking soda)
250ml/8fl oz/1 cup buttermilk

For the filling
2 egg whites
125g/4¼oz/generous ½ cup caster (superfine) sugar
225g/8oz/1 cup unsalted (sweet) butter, softened
40g/1½oz cocoa powder
4–5 drops peppermint extract

For the topping
100g/3¾oz dark (bittersweet) chocolate, melted
24 fresh mint leaves

Preheat the oven to 180°C/350°F/Gas 4. Line two baking trays with baking parchment or silicone mats.

To make the cakes, whisk the butter, sugar and vanilla seeds together until light and creamy. Whisk in the egg. In a separate bowl, sift the flour with the cocoa powder and bicarbonate of soda.

Fold half of the dry ingredients into the butter mixture. Mix in the buttermilk, then add the rest of the dry ingredients and mix together.

Using a piping (pastry) bag fitted with a large plain nozzle, pipe 48 3cm/1¼in rounds of cake mixture 4cm/1½in apart on each baking tray. Bake for 10–12 minutes, or until the cakes bounce back when gently pressed. Transfer to a wire rack to cool.

To make the filling, put the egg whites and sugar in a heatproof bowl and place the bowl over a pan of gently simmering water. Using an electric whisk, whisk the ingredients together until the sugar has dissolved and the mixture is white and hot.

Remove the bowl from the heat and continue to whisk the mixture on high speed until the bottom of the bowl starts to cool down. Turn the speed down to low and whisk in the butter, about 15g/½oz/1 tbsp at a time, making sure that each addition is fully incorporated before adding the next. Gently fold in the sifted cocoa powder and peppermint extract until fully incorporated.

To assemble the pies, place a tablespoon of filling on to the flat side of one cake and top with the flat side of another. Repeat to make 24 pies. When you are ready to serve them, spread a little melted chocolate over the tops, and place a mint leaf on each one.

Energy 238kcal/1001kJ; Protein 3g; Carbohydrate 26g, of which sugars 16g; Fat 14g, of which saturates 9g; Cholesterol 44mg; Calcium 44mg; Fibre 0.5g; Sodium 196mg.

MINTED EARL GREY SORBET

Originally favoured by the Georgians at grand summer balls, this refreshing, slightly tart sorbet is perfect for a lazy afternoon in the garden.

Serves 6

200g/7oz/1 cup caster (superfine) sugar

300ml/½ pint/1¼ cups cold water

1 lemon, well scrubbed

45ml/3 tbsp Earl Grey tea leaves

450ml/¾ pint/2 cups boiling water

1 egg white

30ml/2 tbsp chopped fresh mint leaves

fresh mint sprigs or frosted mint, to decorate

COOK'S TIP

• If you only have Earl Grey tea bags these can be used instead, but add enough to make 450ml/¾ pint/scant 2 cups strong tea.

• Make frosted mint leaves by dipping the leaves in egg white and sprinkling them with caster (superfine) sugar. Leave to dry.

Put the caster sugar and cold water into a saucepan and bring the mixture to the boil, stirring until the sugar has dissolved.

Thinly pare the rind from the lemon so that it falls straight into the pan of syrup. Simmer for 2 minutes then pour into a bowl. Allow to cool, then chill.

Put the tea into a pan and pour on the boiling water. Cover and leave to stand for 5 minutes, then strain into a bowl. Cool, then chill.

By hand: Pour the tea into a plastic tub or similar freezerproof container. Strain in the chilled syrup. Freeze for 4 hours.

Lightly whisk the egg white until just frothy. Scoop the sorbet into a food processor or blender, process until smooth and mix in the mint and egg white. Spoon back into the tub and freeze for 4 hours until firm.

Using an ice cream maker: Combine the tea and syrup and churn the mixture until thick.

Add the mint to the mixture. Lightly whisk the egg white until just frothy, then tip it into the ice cream maker and continue to churn until firm enough to scoop.

Serve in scoops, decorated with a few fresh or frosted mint leaves.

Energy 135kcal/578kJ; Protein 0.8g; Carbohydrate 35.1g, of which sugars 34.8g; Fat 0g, of which saturates 0g; Cholesterol 0mg; Calcium 29mg; Fibre 0g; Sodium 13mg.

PEPPERMINT SWIRL ICE CREAM

Delicately marbled with a pale green tinged syrup, this light and refreshing yogurt ice cream is the perfect recipe for serving after a rich main course.

Serves 6

75g/6 tbsp caster (superfine) sugar
60ml/4 tbsp water
10 large fresh peppermint sprigs
5ml/1 tsp peppermint extract
450 ml/³⁄₄ pint/scant 2 cups double (heavy) cream
a few drops of green food colouring
200ml/7fl oz/scant 1 cup Greek (US strained plain) yogurt
fresh mint leaves, to decorate
sifted icing (confectioners') sugar, to decorate

Put the sugar, water and fresh peppermint sprigs in a small heavy saucepan and heat gently, stirring occasionally, until the sugar has dissolved. Bring to the boil and cook without stirring for about 3 minutes to make a syrup.

Strain the syrup into a bowl and stir in the peppermint extract then leave to cool. Mix half the peppermint mixture with 30ml/1 tbsp of the cream and a few drops of food colouring, then chill until required.

Mix the remaining mint syrup with the remaining cream and the yogurt and pour into a freezerproof container. Freeze for 1 hour until the mixture thickens.

Take the mixture out of the freezer and add a few spoonfuls of the reserved coloured mint cream. Using a metal spoon handle, gently stir the mixture together with five or six strokes until it is marbled. Freeze the ice cream for 2 hours or until it is firm.

Scoop the ice cream into dishes and decorate with mint leaves that have been dusted lightly with sifted icing sugar.

Energy 460kcal/1900kJ; Protein 3.4g;
Carbohydrate 15g, of which sugars 15g; Fat
43.7g, of which saturates 26.8g;
Cholesterol 103mg; Calcium 93mg;
Fibre 0g; Sodium 41mg

PINEAPPLE AND MINT SMOOTHIE

Mint and pineapple make great companions in this light and refreshing, frothy smoothie. Reserve thin segments of pineapple to add to the glass when serving

Serves 2

1 large fresh ripe pineapple,
   about 300g/11oz
30ml/2 tbsp caster (superfine)
   sugar (optional)
500ml/17fl oz/2¼ cups water,
   preferably chilled
small handful fresh mint leaves
250ml/8fl oz/1 cup ice cubes

Peel and chop the pineapple. Put the pineapple chunks, sugar, water, mint leaves (reserve a few to garnish), and ice in a blender. Blend for 3–4 minutes until smooth.

Pour the blended pineapple into tall glasses, topped with a little extra ice, if liked. Decorate with mint leaves and serve each with a long-handled spoon and a slice of pineapple tucked into the glass.

Energy 122kcal/521kJ; Protein 0.7g;
Carbohydrate 31.1g, of which sugars 30.9g;
Fat 0.3g, of which saturates 0g;
Cholesterol 0mg; Calcium 35mg;
Fibre 2g; Sodium 4mg

GARDEN MINT MILKSHAKE

If you can pick mint straight from your garden, all the better as the fresher the mint, the better the flavour. It's infused in a sugar syrup, then blended to a frothy shake with yogurt and creamy milk.

Makes 2 tall glasses
small bunch of fresh mint
*50g/2oz/¼ cup caster
    (superfine) sugar*
*200g/7oz/scant 1 cup natural
    (plain) yogurt*
*200ml/7fl oz/scant 1 cup full
    cream (whole) milk*
15ml/1 tbsp lemon juice
crushed ice cubes
*mint sprigs and icing
    (confectioners') sugar, to
    decorate*

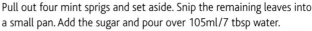

Energy 224kcal/947kJ; Protein 8.4g;
Carbohydrate 38.8g, of which sugars 38.4g;
Fat 4.9g, of which saturates 3.2g;
Cholesterol 15.3mg; Calcium 296mg;
Fibre 0g; Sodium 108mg

Pull out four mint sprigs and set aside. Snip the remaining leaves into a small pan. Add the sugar and pour over 105ml/7 tbsp water.

Heat the mixture, stirring occasionally, until the sugar dissolves, then boil for 2 minutes. Remove from the heat and set aside until cool. Strain the cooled syrup through a sieve into a jug (pitcher), pressing the mint against the side of the sieve with the back of a spoon to extract all the syrup. Pour into a food processor or blender.

Add the yogurt and milk to the syrup and blend until smooth and frothy. Add two of the reserved mint sprigs and lemon juice and blend until the milkshake is specked with tiny green flecks.

Put the ice in tall glasses or tumblers and pour over the milkshake. Dust the mint sprigs with icing sugar and decorate the glasses.

MINT AND APPLE JELLY

When fresh mint is in abundance in the garden why not make your own mint-speckled jelly? It goes particularly well with a delicious dinner of roast lamb.

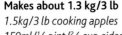

Makes about 1.3 kg/3 lb

1.5kg/3 lb cooking apples
150ml/¼ pint/⅔ cup cider vinegar
750ml/1¼ pints/3 cups water
675g/1½ lb/scant 3½ cups granulated (white) sugar
2 large handfuls fresh mint, chopped
few drops green food colouring, if using

Roughly chop the apples, including cores and skin, and put into a large heavy pan. Add the vinegar and water and bring to the boil. Reduce the heat and simmer the contents for 30 minutes, or until the apples are pulpy.

Pour the fruit and juices into a sterilized jelly bag suspended over a large bowl. Leave to drain for several hours, or until the fruit juices stop dripping.

Measure the juice and pour back into the cleaned pan. For every 600ml/1 pint/2½ cups of juice, add 450g/1 lb/2¼ cups sugar. Slowly bring to the boil, stirring occasionally, until the sugar has completely dissolved. Boil rapidly for 10–15 minutes, or until the setting point is reached (105°C/220°F).

Remove the pan from the heat and skim off any scum from the jelly with a perforated spoon.

Stir in the chopped mint and add a few drops of green food colouring, if you like. Ladle into sterilized dry jars. Cover and seal while hot. Leave to cool.

Store in a cool place out of direct sunlight for up to six months.

Energy 2803kcal/11,963kJ; Protein 5.5g; Carbohydrate 740.7g, of which sugars 740.7g; Fat 0.4g, of which saturates 0g; Cholesterol 0mg; Calcium 401mg; Fibre 6.2g; Sodium 49mg

INDEX